Executive Summary

The United States economy continues to recover from the worst economic crisis since the Great Depression, and while substantial progress has been made, more work remains to boost economic growth and speed job creation. Despite ten consecutive quarters of GDP growth and 8.2 million private sector jobs added since early 2010, the unemployment rate is unacceptably high at 6.7 percent, and far too many families are still struggling to regain the foothold they had prior to the crisis.

The Emergency Unemployment Compensation (EUC) program authorized by Congress in 2008 has provided crucial support to the economy and to millions of Americans who lost jobs through no fault of their own. EUC ended on December 28, 2013[1]. This report argues that failing to extend EUC would be harmful to millions of workers and their families, counterproductive to the economic recovery, and unprecedented in the context of previous extensions to earlier unemployment insurance programs.

Since their inception in 2008, extended unemployment insurance (UI) benefits have provided critical support to millions of workers and their families:

- Over 24 million workers have received extended UI benefits

- Recipients are a diverse group: roughly half have completed at least some college, including 4.8 million with bachelor's degrees or higher

- Including workers' families, over 70 million people have been supported by extended UI benefits, including more than 17 million children

- In 2012 alone, UI benefits lifted an estimated 2.5 million people out of poverty

Millions of workers have lost access to UI benefits because no action has been taken:

- Approximately 1.3 million workers who had been receiving extended UI benefits lost them at the end of 2013

- 3.6 million additional people will be denied access to UI benefits beyond 26 weeks by the end of 2014

Failing to extend EUC would be damaging to the macro-economy and the labor force:

- Failing to extend UI benefits would put a dent in job-seekers' incomes, reducing demand and costing 240,000 jobs in 2014.

---

[1] In all states except New York, the last payable week of EUC benefits will be the week ending December 28. In New York, it will be the week ending December 29.

- Estimates from the Congressional Budget Office and JP Morgan suggest that without an extension of EUC GDP will be .2 to .4 percentage points lower.

- In 2011, CBO found that aid to the unemployed is among the policies with "the largest effects on output and employment per dollar of budgetary cost"

- In over a dozen studies, economists have found that any disincentive to find new work that could result from extended UI benefits is, at most, small

- Expiration of extended UI benefits may also lead some long-term unemployed to stop looking for work and leave the labor force, reducing the number who could eventually find jobs as the economy heals

Failing to extend EUC would be unprecedented in the context of previous extensions to earlier unemployment insurance programs:

- The unemployment rate (6.7% in December) is currently higher than it was at the expiration of all but two previous extended UI benefits programs

- The average duration of unemployment (37.1 weeks in December) is higher than in any month prior to the Great Recession since 1948, and nearly twice as high as it was at the expiration of every previous extended UI benefits program.

- The long-term unemployment rate (2.5% in December) is nearly twice as high as it was at the expiration of every previous extended UI benefits program

- Consistent with previous programs, the EUC program has been gradually phasing down – the median number of weeks one can receive benefits across states is down from a peak of 53 weeks in 2010 to 28.6 weeks at the end of 2013 and 14 weeks under the proposed extension

I.   Introduction

Ten consecutive quarters of economic growth have raised the output of the American economy to an all-time high, more than five percent above its peak before the Great Recession. The labor market has grown steadily as America's resilient businesses have added jobs for 46 consecutive months. Due to the depth of the recession that began in 2007, however, more work must be done to aid workers who continue to struggle to find jobs and to ensure that the economy continues to grow. As of December 2013, 10.4 million workers are unemployed, including 3.9 million who have been out of work for more than 26 weeks.

The Emergency Unemployment Compensation (EUC) program authorized by Congress in 2008 has provided crucial support to the economy and to millions of Americans who lost jobs through no fault of their own. EUC ended on December 28, 2013 at which point approximately 1.3 million workers lost benefits immediately. By the end of 2014 another 3.6 million workers will be denied access to EUC benefits when they exhaust their regular unemployment insurance (UI) benefits before finding employment. As this report details, extending EUC would support these workers and the approximately 9 million others in their families. It would also provide an important boost to economic growth and job creation. Since 1948 Congress has only once allowed extended unemployment benefits to expire with unemployment rates as high as they are now and the long-term unemployment rate is currently nearly twice as high as in any previous month in which benefits expired.

More than 70 million workers and family members have benefitted from the EUC and EB programs since 2008. Direct beneficiaries of Emergency Unemployment Compensation (EUC) represent a broad cross-section of the population: younger and older workers are roughly equally represented; about 40 percent have household incomes, prior to job loss, between $30,000 and $75,000; and while 13 percent did not finish high-school, 20 percent have a four-year college degree, and the remaining two-thirds of the recipients have education through high school or some college. For many of these Americans and their families, EUC was all that stood between them and poverty: the Census Bureau estimates that unemployment benefits lifted 2.5 million people from poverty in 2012 alone and has kept over 11 million out of poverty since 2008.

There is broad agreement amongst economists that the extended unemployment benefits provided to families during times of high unemployment do *not* noticeably reduce incentives for workers to find jobs. For example, a recent study of EUC in the Great Recession finds that extensions raised the unemployment rate at the end of 2010 by only 0.2 percentage points, about 2 percent of the 9.3 percent unemployment rate in that month. Moreover, recent research has shown that whatever disincentive effects may exist, they are even smaller when jobs are scarce as strategic considerations are dominated by the urgent need to find a job. This logic suggests that unemployment benefits should increase when jobs are scarce and contract when the labor market is strong, which is exactly how EUC is currently designed. As state unemployment rates fall, the program essentially is phased down as states are phased out of eligibility for additional weeks of support.

An often overlooked benefit of extended unemployment compensation programs is that these programs keep the long-term unemployed from exiting the labor market since benefits are contingent on continued job-search. Transitions out of the labor force generally occur at a higher rate for those unemployed 27 weeks or more than for those unemployed for shorter periods. After the EUC legislation was enacted in 2008, however, the rate of transition out of the labor force among those who were unemployed for 27 to 52 weeks and those unemployed over a year actually fell to the lowest level on record. Though the job-finding rate is low for the long-term unemployed (currently about 10 percent per month for those unemployed 27 weeks or more), keeping them in the labor market increases the number who eventually do find jobs.

FAILING TO EXTEND UNEMPLOYMENT INSURANCE BENEFITS WILL LEAD MILLIONS OF WORKERS TO LOSE THEIR BENEFITS AND HARM THE RECOVERY:

EUC and EB have been essential for millions of Americans during since 2008.
- 24.3 million Americans have received EUC and EB benefits since the inception of the EUC program in 2008.
- Including other household members, more than 70 million people have benefited from EUC and EB, including over 17 million children.
- UI benefits help people across the income spectrum: Over 40 percent of households that received UI benefits in 2012 but not in 2011 had household income between $30,000 and $75,000 in the year before experiencing the loss of a household member's job.
- In 2012, 2.5 million Americans were lifted from poverty through support from UI.

Without an extension, 4.9 million people will no longer have access to unemployment benefits beyond 26 weeks in 2014.

According to the Congressional Budget Office, EUC is among policies with "the largest effects on output and employment per dollar of budgetary cost." The benefits unemployed Americans receive are often spent immediately on necessary goods like food, clothing, and shelter, supporting local businesses in their communities. Without an extension, the Council of Economic Advisers estimates that the economy will generate 240,000 fewer jobs by the end of 2014.

The Administration has supported reforms to the unemployment insurance system, and the last EUC extension created opportunities for states to improve the program and test new strategies to help get the long-term unemployed back to work. The administration supports a variety of reforms to the UI system that help workers find jobs quicker. It also expanded "work-sharing" programs across the country, which will help prevent layoffs by encouraging struggling employers to reduce hours for workers rather than laying them off. Additionally, for the first time, the reforms allowed the long-term unemployed who were receiving federal benefits to start their own businesses while providing support to states to expand entrepreneurship programs.

The progress made since the depths of the recession in 2010 is a testament to the resilience of the American economy and the American people. Yet more must be done. Extending EUC will enable beneficiaries to search for jobs that utilize their skills, continue to support their families, and support job creation and economic growth in their communities.

II.   Background

President Bush signed extended unemployment insurance benefits into effect in June 2008 when the unemployment rate was 5.6 percent and little additional increase was expected, the long-term unemployment rate was 1.0 percent and the average duration of unemployment was 17.1 weeks. Today, as of December 2013, the unemployment rate is 6.7 percent, the long-term unemployment rate is 2.5 percent and the average duration of unemployment is 37.1 weeks, considerably longer than the 26-week duration of regular UI benefits prevailing in most states. These statistics, combined with the historical patterns of UI extensions, point logically to the importance of Congress continuing extended benefits through EUC.

Unemployment Insurance (UI) is a joint Federal-State program that provides income support to workers who have lost a job. Nearly all full-time and some part-time workers who meet basic criteria are eligible for UI. More than 60 percent of all Americans benefit from income from unemployment insurance by the time they reach their 50s, either as a direct beneficiary or by being married to one. Weekly UI payments for eligible unemployed workers are determined by their past wages, up to a maximum weekly benefit. Program parameters vary across states, but weekly benefits in 2013 averaged a little over $300, replacing about half of UI recipients' lost earnings. Unemployed workers typically qualify for up to 26 weeks of benefits, as long as they continue to search for work. In an economy with normal labor demand, one would expect most unemployed workers to find a job within this time frame; in periods of high unemployment, however, finding a job may take longer.

Since 1972, unemployment benefits have been extended in states experiencing high and rising unemployment through the Extended Benefits (EB) program, a joint Federal-State program. When state unemployment rates reach specific thresholds and are elevated relative to their level over the past several years, the EB program allows states to provide 13 or 20 weeks of additional benefits with the Federal government paying half of the cost. In 2009, Congress provided for 100 percent Federal funding of EB to pay individuals who had exhausted their regular UI and EUC benefits, and later loosened the triggers governing state eligibility for EB.[2] However, because unemployment has been falling for some time, no states currently qualify for the EB.

---

[2] A state is required to offer EB if its insured unemployment rate (IUR) exceeds 5 percent and is at least 20 percent higher than in each of the last three years, but this condition is currently not satisfied in any state. The same is true of the alternative optional trigger that the state IUR exceeds 6 percent. In most cases, for a state to qualify for EB, its total unemployment rate (TUR) must exceed the trigger value shown in Appendix Table 2 and this state TUR must be higher than it was either one year or two years earlier. Under the most recent benefits extension, the "look back" period for EB was extended temporarily to three years rather than two years, making more states eligible to offer EB benefits.

In every recession since 1957, the Federal government has passed legislation to provide extended benefits to buttress the regular unemployment insurance program.[3] These extended benefits are particularly valuable in times of persistent unemployment when the conditions for EB to be triggered are no longer satisfied, as currently. The Emergency Unemployment Compensation (EUC) program that just expired was created by Congress in June 2008, in recognition of the fact that unemployed workers would struggle to find jobs during the downturn. At its inception, EUC provided an additional 13 weeks of federally financed compensation in all states to eligible individuals who had exhausted their regular UI benefits. As the labor market weakened, Congress extended and expanded the program several times. At its most generous, in early 2012, the programs combined to provide long-term unemployed in the highest unemployment states with 99 weeks of benefits. The Middle Class Tax Relief and Job Creation Act, signed in February 2012, legislated staged decreases in the maximum benefit duration.

The most recent renewal of the EUC legislation was signed in January 2013. The program offered four "tiers" of EUC through which unemployed workers were eligible, conditional on their state's unemployment rate. All four tiers of benefits were available only in the states with the highest unemployment rates, those with unemployment at or above 9%. In these states, a total of 73 weeks of benefits were available and workers could move sequentially through the available tiers as long as they remained jobless and continued searching for a job. As the unemployment rate in a state fell, the number of weeks of extended unemployment benefits also declined, with fewer tiers available. As states unemployment rates declined from below 9 percent, states lost access to 10 weeks of benefits. When the states' unemployment rate went below 7 percent, they lost access to another 9 weeks; finally as it fell below 6 percent they lost access to another 14 weeks. Every state, with the exception of North Carolina, had access to at least 14 additional weeks of coverage through the EUC system. (North Carolina forfeited federal EUC funding by reducing the average weekly benefit amount, violating federal law which forced the termination of the EUC program.) Appendix Table 2 shows the different tiers of benefits for which workers may be eligible under the regular UI program, EUC and EB, depending on state law and the unemployment rate in the state.

Because the EUC system was designed to phase down when prosperous economic times returned, the median number of EUC weeks available to a long-term unemployed person fell from almost 36 weeks at the beginning of 2013 to 28.6 at the end of the year. By the time the national unemployment rate falls to 6.5%, which it is projected to do in mid-2015, the Department of Labor projects the median number of weeks of EUC available would fall to 14 under renewed legislation, as shown in Figure 1. Yet, it is important to realize that behind this median estimate lie important differences across states: Figure 1 also shows the longer duration of benefits that would remain for a state projected to have a relatively high unemployment rate (higher than 90 percent of states). By renewing EUC we are able to provide continued support to workers in the states with the most need.

---

[3] The only exception is the short recession during 1980, which was followed by a deeper recession beginning in July 1981. Congress passed an unemployment insurance extension in September 1982 that can be viewed as a response to the combined effects of the two recessions.

Figure 1: Historical and Projected EUC Weeks Available at Median and 90th Percentile

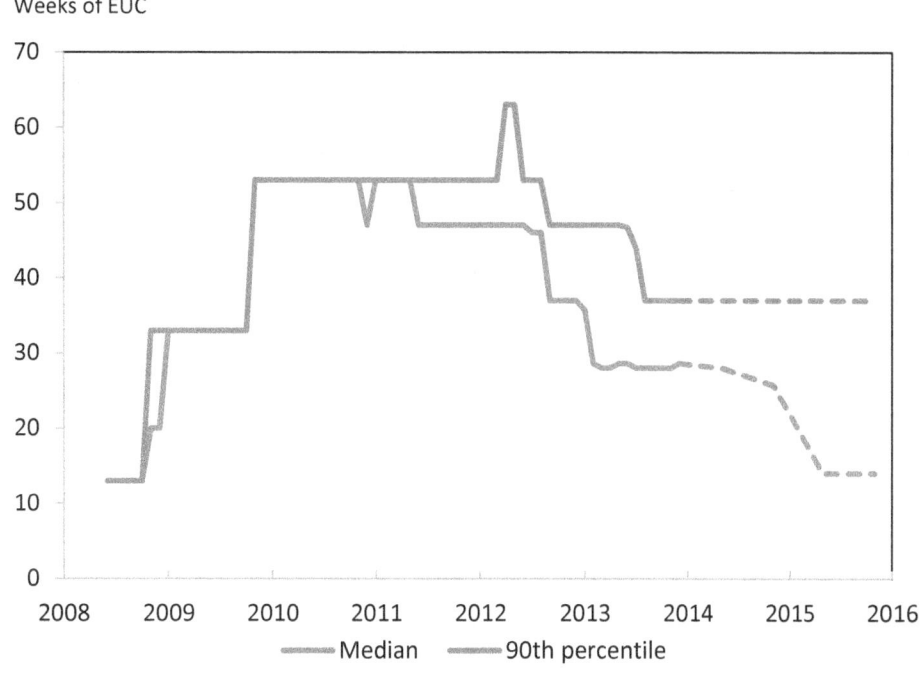

Weeks of EUC

Since 1948, when official monthly unemployment rates first became available, special extended benefits have been provided to long-term unemployed workers in 72 percent of the months in which the national unemployment rate was at the current rate of 6.7 percent or higher. Figure 2 shows that it is not uncommon for extended benefits to have been available for unemployment rates under 7 percent.

Figure 2: Share of Months since 1948 in which Special Extended Benefits Paid, By Unemployment Rate

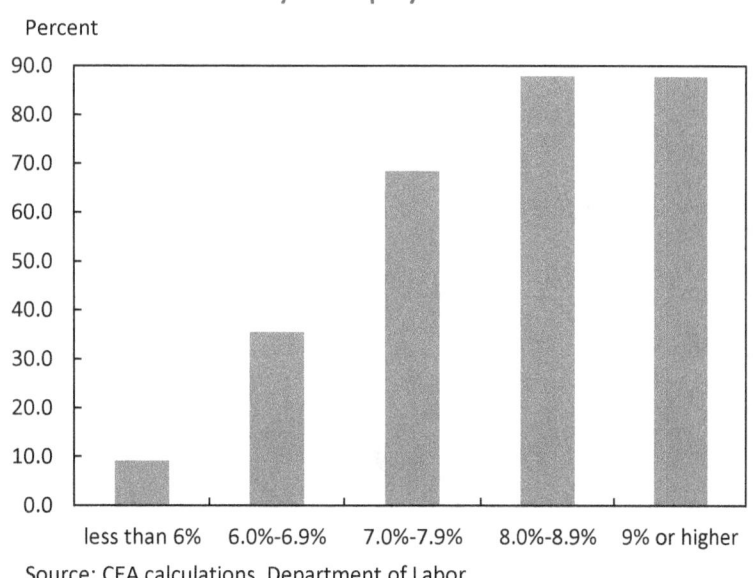

Percent

Source: CEA calculations, Department of Labor

7

In only two prior cases has Congress allowed special extended benefits to expire when the unemployment rate was as high as it is today. Moreover, the long-term unemployment rate is nearly twice as high today as in any prior month when extended benefits were allowed to expire. For example, during the recovery from the 1981-82 recession, the most severe postwar recession before 2007, the extensions passed under President Reagan lasted until June 1985, by which time the economy had made a sizeable recovery from its trough. Moreover, as shown in Figure 3, the average duration of unemployment is currently 37.1 weeks, higher than at any point in history prior the Great Recession and far above the next highest level of 19.8 weeks in a month when EUC benefits were allowed to expired. Table 1 reports the eight time periods since 1956 that special extended benefits have been offered. For each, it shows the month the recession ended, the month the special extended benefits program expired, the unemployment rates and average duration of unemployment in that month. Appendix Table 1 details all special extended benefits programs since the Temporary Unemployment Compensation program of 1958.

Figure 3: Long-Term Unemployment Rate and the Availability of Temporary Extended Federal Unemployment Insurance Programs

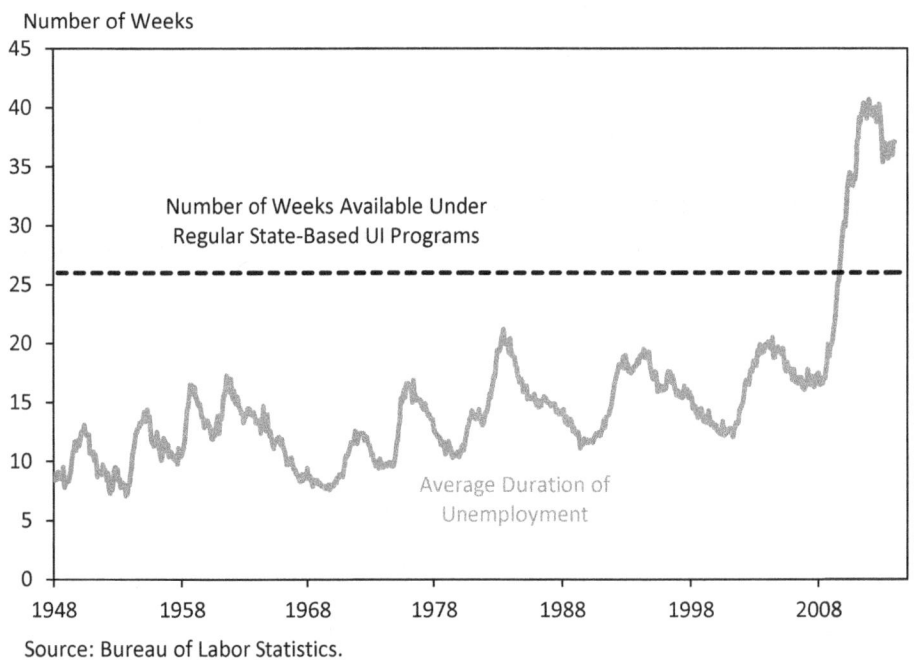

Source: Bureau of Labor Statistics.

The last week for which EUC could be claimed was the week ending December 28, 2013. Those receiving EUC at that time were immediately cut off. Without an extension, workers receiving

Table 1: Unemployment Rates and Average Duration in Months in Which Special Extended Benefits Program Have Expired

Official End of Recession	Month in Which Special Extended Benefits Program Expired	Unemployment Rate at Expiration of Special Benefits Program	Long-term Unemployment Rate at Expiration of Special Benefits Program	Average Duration of Unemployment at Expiration of Special Benefits Program
Apr-58	Apr-59	5.2%	0.9%	14.9
Feb-61	Apr-62	5.6%	0.9%	14.9
Nov-70	Mar-73	4.9%	0.4%	10.6
Mar-75	Nov-77	6.8%	0.9%	13.6
Nov-82	Mar-85	7.2%	1.2%	16.1
Mar-91	Feb-94	6.6%	1.3%	19.0
Nov-01	Dec-03	5.7%	1.3%	19.8
Jun-09	Dec-13	6.7% (Dec. 2013)	2.5% (Dec. 2013)	37.1 (Dec. 2013)

Source: Department of Labor, and CEA Calculations.

regular UI during that week and those who become unemployed subsequently will not receive additional benefits if they exhaust their regular UI (26 weeks in most, but not all states). The last time most workers were eligible for only 26 weeks of benefits the unemployment rate was 5.4 percent.

Finally, Figure 4 shows that with the end of EUC, the share of the unemployed whose families receive support from jobless benefits has likely fallen to the lowest on record (this data will be released next month). On average, during the 12 months ending in November of 2013, 26 percent of unemployed workers received jobless benefits through regular programs, compared to 36 percent on average from 1986 to the beginning of the Great Recession in December 2007. EUC provided benefits to an additional 12 percent of the unemployed in the 12 months ending in November 2013.

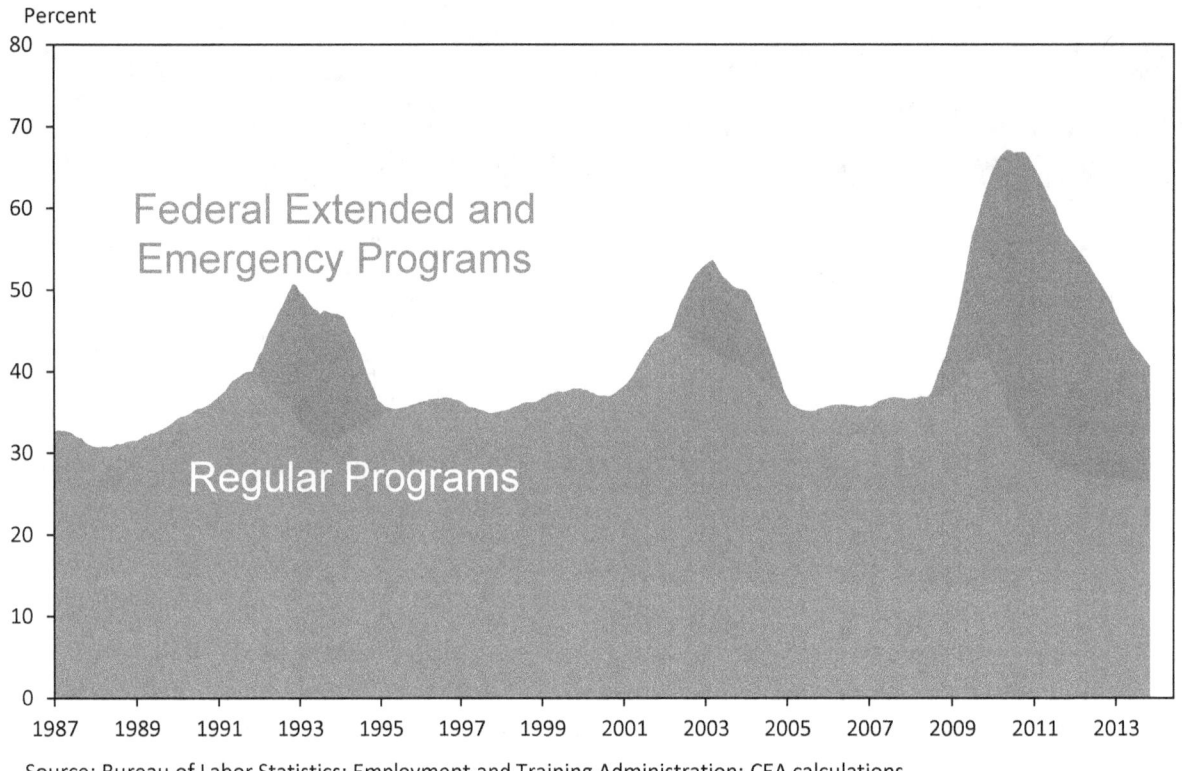

Figure 4: Share of Unemployed Workers Receiving Jobless Benefits Based on 12-Month Moving Average of Not Seasonally Adjusted Data, As of November 2013

Source: Bureau of Labor Statistics; Employment and Training Administration; CEA calculations.

III.   Extended Benefits have Helped Millions of Americans

Extended unemployment insurance benefits have provided crucial support to millions of American workers and their families. Figure 5 shows the total number of job seekers that have benefited from earnings replacement through either EB or EUC. In 2008, the year EUC was

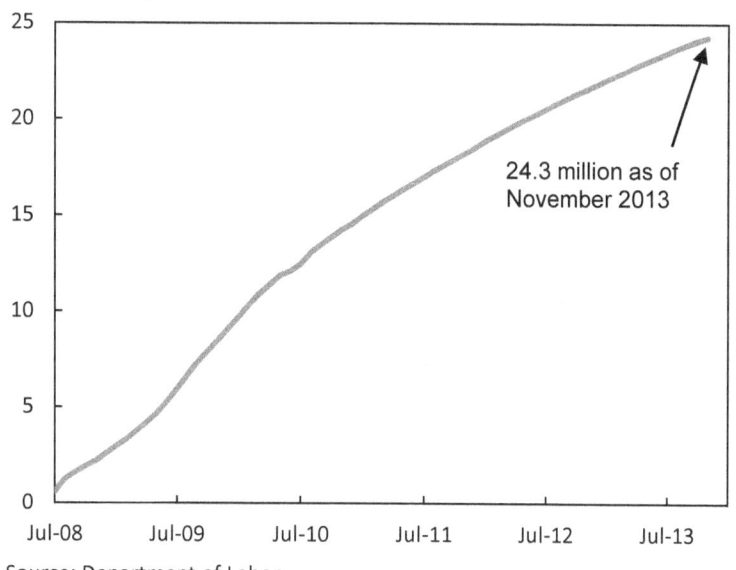

Figure 5: Number of People Receiving EUC/EB Benefits (Cumulative)

Millions of recipients

24.3 million as of November 2013

Source: Department of Labor

enacted, approximately 2 million workers received benefits. As the recession deepened and unemployment continued to rise until January of 2010, more and more laid-off workers who were unable to find jobs in the first 26 weeks of unemployment moved into these programs. While unemployment has been falling steadily since, it has been falling less for those with longer unemployment durations and so more workers have relied on EUC and EB for support. As of September 2013, 23.9 million workers had received EUC/EB benefits. Table 2 provides details on the number of unemployed people aided by EUC/EB benefits in each state.

Counting only the job seekers directly receiving unemployment insurance payments leads to a dramatic understatement of the number of Americans helped by unemployment insurance, since benefits provide income support for all members of the households in which recipients live. In addition to the 24.3 million direct beneficiaries, another 29.0 million adults living with a beneficiary have been helped, along with 17.2 million children in households with beneficiaries. In total, more than 70 million Americans have been aided by EUC/EB since July of 2008.

Table 2: Number of People Receiving EUC/EB Benefits (Cumulative), by State

State	Number of People Who Have Received EUC Benefits from January 2008 through November 2013	State	Number of People Who Have Received EUC Benefits from January 2008 through November 2013
Alabama	282,619	Nebraska	106,220
Alaska	50,682	Nevada	302,539
Arizona	394,996	New Hampshire	58,085
Arkansas	174,884	New Jersey	1,093,444
California	3,224,558	New Mexico	97,769
Colorado	362,423	New York	1,774,471
Connecticut	337,796	North Carolina	1,058,783
Delaware	69,642	North Dakota	25,816
D.C.	62,534	Ohio	800,091
Florida	1,577,376	Oklahoma	178,768
Georgia	868,428	Oregon	383,563
Hawaii	70,554	Pennsylvania	1,457,861
Idaho	101,379	Puerto Rico	198,789
Illinois	1,143,481	Rhode Island	101,232
Indiana	609,363	South Carolina	399,243
Iowa	232,044	South Dakota	11,211
Kansas	205,751	Tennessee	457,339
Kentucky	218,394	Texas	1,228,102
Louisiana	176,223	Utah	132,838
Maine	82,440	Vermont	33,751
Maryland	193,160	Virgin Islands	9,384
Massachusetts	674,513	Virginia	371,183
Michigan	967,963	Washington	276,404
Minnesota	398,032	West Virginia	100,050
Mississippi	189,006	Wisconsin	435,463
Missouri	405,881	Wyoming	32,077
Montana	80,609	US Total	24,279,207

Source: Department of Labor

EUC benefits provide assistance to a wide variety of people. In 2012, 19.6% of EUC beneficiaries were African American, and 15.6% were Hispanic. More than half have completed at least some college, with 25.2% of 2012 beneficiaries having completed a bachelor's degree or higher, a share that has increased over time as workers seek additional training. Job-seekers of all ages have benefitted from EUC, including those early in their careers; more than 27% of EUC beneficiaries have been 34 years old or younger in each year since the beginning of the recession. The support provided by EUC extends beyond beneficiaries themselves, as 77.8% lived in households with at least one other adult in 2012, and 38.5% lived in households with children.

Figure 6: Total EUC Recipients since July 2008, by Characteristics

Total	24,279,207
Household Structure	
Single adult, no children	3,997,329
Single adult, with children	1,522,472
Multiple adults, no children	11,220,387
Multiple adults, with children	7,539,020
Household Income	
Less than $30,000	11,538,425
$30,000 to $74,999	9,910,264
$75,000 and up	1,590,387
Education	
Less than high school	3,460,337
High school	8,503,079
Some college	5,109,807
Associate's degree	2,615,103
Bachelor's degree or higher	4,590,882

Source: CEA Calculations, Current Population Survey, Department of Labor.
Note: Includes beneficiaries through November 2013. 2013 beneficiaries are assumed to have the same characteristics as 2012 beneficiaries. The sum of beneficiaries by income group does not equal the total number of beneficiaries because some CPS respondents did not provide their household income for 2008. This Figure is updated relative to our December 2013 report to reflect new analyses that affect the estimated distribution of EUC beneficiaries across categories.

In each of the first eleven months of 2013, an average of 228,000 people exhausted their UI benefits each month and became EUC recipients. This represents a 15.7 percent decrease from 2012 when 270,000 people were entering EUC every month. At expiration, 1.3 million long-term unemployed workers received EUC (virtually no job-seekers are currently receiving EB). This represents a significant decrease compared to the 2.1 million people who were receiving EUC or EB benefits when the program was last extended in December 2012. Total EUC and EB benefit payments in the first eleven months of 2013 averaged $1.9 billion per month, and in November 2013, the last month for which data are available, total spending on EUC benefits was $1.3 billion. This compares to the average of $3.3 billion in total benefits paid monthly in 2012.

While unemployment has fallen steadily since 2010 and has done so dramatically in some areas of the country, many states are still experiencing extremely high levels of unemployment. As of

November 2013, 3 states and Puerto Rico have unemployment rates above 9 percent, and an additional 24 states, the District of Columbia and the Virgin Islands have unemployment rates above 7 percent. While the economy clearly is healing, the need for substantial assistance to unemployed workers also clearly remains large especially given the high-fraction of long-term unemployed amongst job-seekers.

IV.   Labor Market Effects of Extending Unemployment Benefits

In choosing the optimal unemployment insurance policy, policymakers must weigh competing costs and benefits. On the one hand, some argue that extending benefits may dull the incentives for unemployed workers to exert effort to search for another job, leading to increased unemployment—the so-called "moral-hazard" effect. But on the other hand, providing benefits gives families income that can in the limit keep them from poverty but more generally can help them to finance a longer job search that might ultimately result in a job better matched with their talents, resulting in higher overall labor market productivity—what Chetty (2008) terms the "liquidity effect."

Economists have researched these tradeoffs extensively for over 20 years, producing a wealth of evidence on the topic (Katz and Meyer 1990, Meyer 1990, Card and Levine 2000). In a recent editorial, economist Raj Chetty summarizes these studies as follows:

> *"Nearly a dozen economic studies have analyzed this question by comparing unemployment rates in states that have extended unemployment benefits with those in states that do not. … These studies have uniformly found that a 10-week extension in unemployment benefits raises the average amount of time people spend out of work by at most one week. This simple, unassailable finding implies that policy makers can extend unemployment benefits to provide assistance to those out of work without substantially increasing unemployment rates (Chetty 2013)"*

In his work, Chetty (2008) shows that the beneficial impact of helping liquidity constrained unemployed workers more than outweighs the moral hazard effect. Indeed, he finds hardly any evidence of a moral hazard effect once the liquidity effect is recognized. This finding is confirmed by recent work by Rothstein (2011), who finds minimal impacts of extensions to EUC and EB during the Great Recession on job search intensity. Finally, while economists have found only small disincentive effects of UI extensions, recent research shows that the effect of UI on job search behavior is even smaller in recessions as the moral hazard effect shrinks when jobs are scarce (Kroft and Notowidigdo 2011, Schmieder, von Wachter, and Bender 2012). In contrast, the benefits due to the liquidity effect—allowing households to avoid dramatic declines in consumption and allowing job-seekers to search long enough for a suitable job—increase, arguing for longer benefit durations when the labor market is weak.

An often overlooked benefit of extended unemployment compensation programs is that these programs tend to prevent the long-term unemployed from exiting the labor market. As can be seen in Figure 7, transitions out of the labor force generally occur at a higher rate for those unemployed 27 weeks or more than for those unemployed for shorter periods. After extended benefits legislation was enacted in 2008, however, the rate of transition out of the labor force among those who were unemployed for 27 to 52 weeks and those unemployed over a year actually fell below that of groups with shorter durations of unemployment. In a recent econometric analysis, Rothstein (2011) finds that the majority of the modest increase in unemployment caused by the availability of extended benefits is attributable primarily to lowering the number of people who leave the labor force rather than to lowering the number who become employed. Though the job-finding rate is low for the long-term unemployed (currently about 10 percent per month for those unemployed 27 weeks or more), keeping them in the labor market increases the number who eventually do find jobs.

Figure 7: Monthly Transitions from Unemployment to Not in the Labor Force by Duration of Unemployment, January 2003 to March 2013

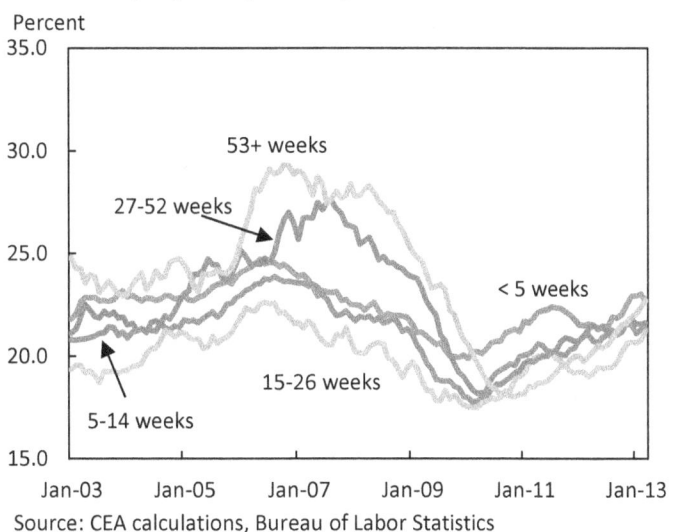

Source: CEA calculations, Bureau of Labor Statistics

The extended benefits programs do not appear to have had a differential impact on the relative job-finding rates of unemployed persons who have been out of work for different lengths of time. As shown in Figure 8, job-finding rates are consistently lower for those who have been unemployed longer, but the rates for the different cohorts delineated by unemployment duration have stayed roughly parallel since 2003.

Figure 8: Monthly Transitions from Unemployment to Employment by Duration of Unemployment, January 2003 to March 2013

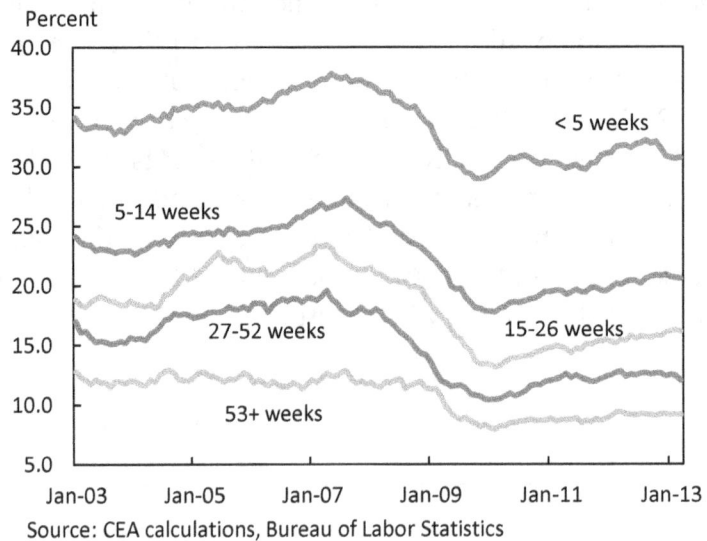

Source: CEA calculations, Bureau of Labor Statistics

In contrast to this strong consensus among peer-reviewed studies conducted over the past 20 years, two recent working papers cited by the House Ways and Means Committee—Hagedorn et al. (2013) and Mitman and Rabinovitch (2012)—argue that recent extensions to the UI program have significantly impeded the labor market recovery after the Great Recession. The papers concede that UI benefits have only small disincentive effects on workers' search effort, but argue instead that benefit extensions discourage job creation by firms by putting upward pressure on wages, thus making job creation less profitable. This increases unemployment, they argue, since for any amount of search effort there are simply fewer jobs to be had than would have been the case had benefits not been extended.

This argument and the model it stems from have important inconsistencies. The model in Hagedorn et al. (2013) assumes that UI affects wages of both incumbent workers and job seekers by improving the bargaining position of workers by raising their expected income if they decline a job offer. As noted by Robert Hall (2013), however, incumbents would need to quit in order to "take advantage" of higher unemployment income and workers who quit their jobs are in fact not eligible for UI. Given this, the paper's finding that UI extensions increase wages for incumbents (Table 5) is not in fact consistent with their model or other standard models of wage determination. Going beyond this inconsistency, the model also ignores important features of the recession such as a dramatic spike in layoffs in late 2008. That fact notwithstanding, the paper claims that "most of the persistent increase in unemployment during the Great Recession can be accounted for by the unprecedented extensions of unemployment benefit eligibility." Taken at face value, this suggests some omitted factor that must have changed contemporaneously with EUC extensions to offset the huge adverse employment impact those layoffs should have produced. This is highly implausible.

The empirics of Hagedorn et al. paper are also problematic. The paper attempts to isolate the effect of UI extensions by studying differences in unemployment in contiguous counties on opposite sides of a state boundary with differing unemployment benefit durations. The idea behind this research design is that the two counties will have similar populations and experience similar economic shocks, and so should have similar unemployment in the absence of policy differences. Unfortunately, the Bureau of Labor Statistics data used in the paper cannot support such an analysis since they are derived from a model that uses state level variables to predict county level employment. Thus, even if unemployment rates vary continuously across geography, measured rates will jump at the state border.

Mitman and Rabinovitch (2012) note on the title page of their draft, available on the web, that the study is preliminary and incomplete. It is nevertheless worth noting that the nature of the methodology is such that positive effects on aggregate demand of UI and EUC are not taken into consideration, eliminating by assumption the key channel through which EUC can aid economic growth and the recovery. Furthermore, the authors do not in this early draft take into account that extensions to UI benefits come into effect only when unemployment is high, whether through the Extended Benefits automatic triggers or through legislation. Had the recent labor market recoveries been as robust in the absence of EUC as the authors find in their simulations, it is unlikely EUC would have been introduced.

V.   Unemployment Benefits Support Economic Growth

In a 2011 study, the CBO found that increasing aid to the unemployed is among the policies that would have "the largest effects on output and employment per dollar of budgetary cost" (CBO 2011). Since unemployment benefits tend to flow to people who need the dollars for necessary expenses, the literature suggests that increased spending from unemployment compensation happens very soon after the outlay of federal dollars. In contrast to many other job creation programs that involve longer lags between Federal spending and economic benefits, extensions to UI are "both timely and cost-effective in spurring … economic activity and employment" (CBO 2011).

In addition to providing income insurance for families, unemployment compensation also helps the economy as a whole (Auerbach and Feenberg 2000). Job loss results in a significant decline in income and therefore consumption for workers and their families. This drop in consumption means a loss of demand for businesses, amplifying the original drop in aggregate demand. Unemployment compensation is an automatic stabilizer; it mitigates the impact of a recession on the broader economy because unemployed workers—whose income has been severely reduced due to the job loss—tend to spend their benefits rather than save them. Economic research examining UI suggests that, in the absence of the UI system, a typical family whose head of household becomes unemployed would spend 22 percent less on food—as compared to the 7 percent drop that is actually observed because of the help of the UI system (Gruber 1997). More recent, preliminary, work by Rothstein and Valetta (2013) finds similarly that household income falls by about 16 percent when UI benefits are exhausted, with the drop in

UI income partially compensated by slightly increased participation in SNAP and other programs.

In recent years, unemployment compensation has had a significant role in maintaining household income levels. Council of Economic Advisers (CEA) calculations based on data from the Current Population Survey show that, from 2007 to 2010, the share of households receiving income from unemployment compensation rose from 4.1 percent to 9.6 percent and the average amount received by these households increased from $4,400 to $8,343. As the economy improved the share of households receiving UI fell to 6.6 percent, and the average amount received fell to $6,681, but both figures are still more than 50 percent higher than their pre-recession levels. Previous research suggests that recipients tend to understate their unemployment compensation by up to one-third (Meyer, Mok, and Sullivan 2009), so these are likely to be lower bound estimates of the effect of unemployment insurance on household income.

In addition, unemployment is a leading cause of mortgage defaults, and the income provided by unemployment insurance helps avert foreclosures—giving much needed support to our housing market (Foote et al. 2009).

Because the EUC and EB programs support hundreds of thousands of jobs and increase economic activity significantly, they also generate partially offsetting tax revenue for the Federal government (through income and payroll taxes) and help state and local budgets by increasing sales tax revenues. Additionally, without the income support from extended unemployment compensation, many families would need to draw on other programs such as the Supplemental Nutrition Assistance Program (SNAP, formerly known as food stamps), Temporary Assistance to Needy Families (TANF) and SSDI.[4]

In short, as a form of insurance, the Federal unemployment compensation programs provide important income support for workers and their families during periods of job loss, but they have substantial benefits to the broader economy as well. As a result, the net cost to the Federal government is less than the official cost that is scored for these programs when they are considered in isolation.[5]

VI. The Cost of Inaction

The EUC program expired on January 1, 2014. The last week for which EUC could be claimed in most states was the week ending December 28, 2013; there was no phase out. Furthermore, without an extension, workers receiving regular UI during that week and those who become unemployed subsequently will not be able to claim EUC if they exhaust their regular UI (26 weeks in most states, but 18-25 in seven states, and 28-30 in two states). Millions of long-term

---

[4] Unemployment benefits are included in the income calculation used to determine SNAP eligibility. Therefore, without unemployment benefits, more families would be eligible to receive SNAP.
[5] For example, the Congressional Budget Office (2008) noted this effect in its cost analysis of the Emergency Extended Unemployment Compensation Act of 2008.

unemployed workers are being affected, despite the fact that the unemployment rate still stands at 6.7 percent and the average currently on-going spell of unemployment has lasted more than 37 weeks.

Figure 9 illustrates the number of unemployed who would be affected by the failure to extend EUC. At expiration, 1.3 million abruptly lost EUC payments, receiving their last benefit check in the last days of December 2013 or in early January 2014. In the first six months of 2014, a further 1.9 million unemployed would exhaust regular benefits, but be unable to transition to EUC. An additional 1.6 million unemployed would suffer the same fate in the second six months of 2014, making a total of 4.9 million affected people.

Figure 9: Projected Number of Unemployed Denied Benefits if EUC is Not Extended (Cumulative)

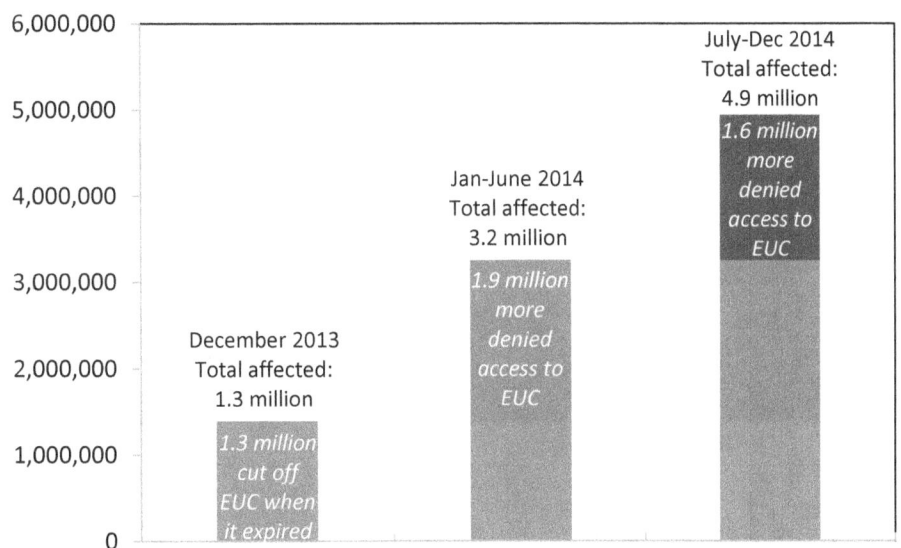

These benefit losses will have devastating consequences for many of the long-term unemployed and their families. While the weekly benefit amount is not large, it is enough to keep many families out of poverty. In 2012, 2.5 million people were pulled out of poverty by unemployment compensation, of whom 600,000 were children. By the end of 2014, almost 3.6 million children will be directly affected by the loss of benefits by someone in their household. All told, 11.4 million people have been kept out of poverty by unemployment insurance since the EUC program began.

These effects will not be limited geographically. Every state except North Carolina offered EUC benefits before the program expired, so people in every state but one who lost their eligibility. State-by-state projections of the number of additional people who would be affected by the termination of EUC from expiry through the end of 2014 are shown in Table 3: these numbers include those whose EUC benefits are terminated and those unable to transition on to EUC.

Table 3: Projected Number of Unemployed Affected in 2014 if EUC is Not Extended (Cumulative)

State	Affected unemployed	State	Affected unemployed
Alabama	48,533	Nebraska	17,564
Alaska	24,765	Nevada	59,433
Arizona	63,899	New Hampshire	8,562
Arkansas	40,422	New Jersey	257,975
California	863,923	New Mexico	25,664
Colorado	72,961	New York	381,511
Connecticut	84,271	North Carolina	0
Delaware	13,783	North Dakota	8,355
District of Columbia	18,089	Ohio	127,669
Florida	256,299	Oklahoma	32,940
Georgia	167,305	Oregon	76,127
Hawaii	13,391	Pennsylvania	266,311
Idaho	20,240	Puerto Rico	79,145
Illinois	244,739	Rhode Island	22,080
Indiana	70,028	South Carolina	52,415
Iowa	36,223	South Dakota	1,702
Kansas	35,535	Tennessee	77,843
Kentucky	53,121	Texas	286,622
Louisiana	30,961	Utah	20,662
Maine	18,522	Vermont	5,193
Maryland	84,482	Virgin Islands	3,574
Massachusetts	160,557	Virginia	70,406
Michigan	193,473	Washington	104,923
Minnesota	67,114	West Virginia	24,992
Mississippi	36,121	Wisconsin	99,885
Missouri	88,033	Wyoming	6,939
Montana	14,815		

Source: Department of Labor

The resulting decline in benefit payments will force millions of households to reduce consumption in the short term, causing significant adverse effects on aggregate demand and thus on employment. At the time of the extension for 2012, the CBO (2011) projected that, compared to allowing extending benefits to expire, an extension could have the cumulative effect in 2012 and 2013 of raising output by up to $1.9 billion and employment by up to 19,000 full-time equivalent job-years for every billion dollars of budgetary spending – the largest impact of any policy they examined. Using the same method the Department of Labor has estimated the effect of extending EUC for one year, maintaining the current program rules, on the number of job-years, compared to what would happen if benefits were allowed to expire.

The calculation involves using a standard fiscal multiplier applied to the total amount of anticipated benefit payments and considers only the effects of EUC on employment that operates through the effect on aggregate demand. While there is unavoidable uncertainty about the precise effects, DOL estimates that extended benefits would save as many as 240,000 additional job-years cumulatively by the end of 2014.

To estimate the state-by-state employment impacts of extending EUC financing for another year, the estimated national employment effect was allocated across states based on each state's share of total extended benefit payments. As illustrated in Figure 10, this translates into hundreds or, in most cases, thousands of job-years in every state in the country, compared to what would be expected if benefits were not extended.

Figure 10: Estimated Number of Jobs Saved by EUC Extension through the Fourth Quarter of 2014, by State

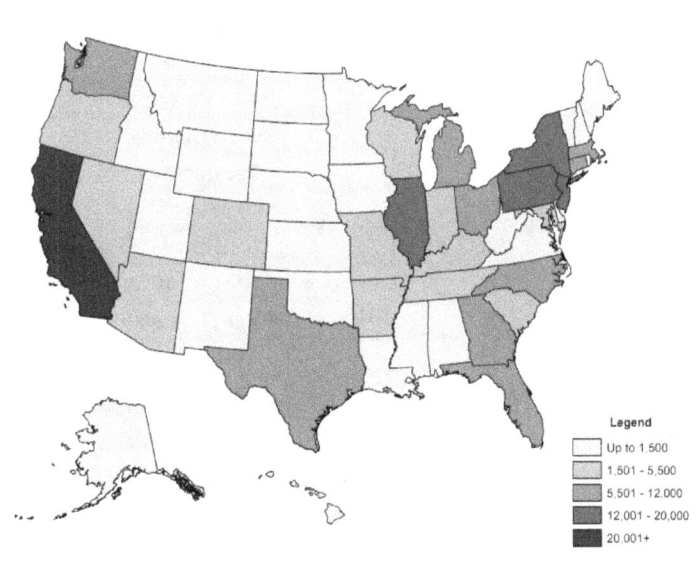

Sources: Department of Labor, CEA calculations

State-by-state estimates of job-years saved through the end of 2014 are reported in Table 4. The estimates show, for example, that EUC and EB would save more than 10,000 jobs in Florida, Illinois, Pennsylvania, and Texas; more than 19,000 jobs in New York; and nearly 46,000 jobs in California.

Table 4: Impact on Employment of a Failure to Extend EUC, by State

State	Estimated Number of Jobs Saved by EUC Extension Through End of 2014	State	Estimated Number of Jobs Saved by EUC Extension Through End of 2014
Alabama	1,083	Nebraska	456
Alaska	1,212	Nevada	2,953
Arizona	1,938	New Hampshire	225
Arkansas	2,088	New Jersey	19,660
California	46,441	New Mexico	989
Colorado	3,571	New York	19,826
Connecticut	5,788	North Carolina	7,629
Delaware	505	North Dakota	146
District of Columbia	993	Ohio	6,535
Florida	10,109	Oklahoma	659
Georgia	5,876	Oregon	3,829
Hawaii	585	Pennsylvania	15,200
Idaho	522	Puerto Rico	1,691
Illinois	13,345	Rhode Island	1,284
Indiana	3,406	South Carolina	1,892
Iowa	824	South Dakota	31
Kansas	846	Tennessee	2,276
Kentucky	3,151	Texas	11,766
Louisiana	726	Utah	542
Maine	675	Vermont	118
Maryland	3,462	Virgin Islands	238
Massachusetts	7,067	Virginia	1,477
Michigan	8,450	Washington	6,183
Minnesota	1,078	West Virginia	1,173
Mississippi	1,412	Wisconsin	5,185
Missouri	2,456	Wyoming	134
Montana	295	US Total	240,000

Source: Department of Labor

VII. Other UI-Related Reforms and Innovations Have Also Benefited Workers

The **American Recovery and Reinvestment Act of 2009** set aside $7 billion to incentivize states to modernize their UI systems and update eligibility rules to reflect the state of the labor market. To receive an incentive payment, a state had to adopt an alternative base-period, a measure that allows workers to qualify based on their most recent earnings, to determine eligibility. States also had to complete at least two of the following:

- pay UI to individuals seeking only part-time work;

- make eligible workers who quit their job because of family responsibilities, leave because of a domestic violence or sexual assault, or accompany a spouse who moves to a new job;
- extend benefits to workers in approved training programs who exhaust regular UI; or,
- provide a dependent allowance.

Overall, states received $4.4 billion of ARRA funds for their UI Modernization efforts. The law prompted 41 states to make nearly 100 reforms to their UI programs. Numerous states extended UI eligibility to workers whose job loss was due to compelling family circumstances, with 13 states adding coverage for domestic violence, 14 choosing to add coverage to care for a sick family member, and 16 extending coverage to a relocating spouse.

The **Middle Class Tax Act of 2012** also made a number of innovative reforms to the UI program to help workers return to employment faster. First, the Act made participation in reemployment services (RES) and reemployment and eligibility assessments (REAs) a requirement for EUC claimants to be eligible. These types of assessments and services have been shown to speed the return of claimants to work and are more than cost effective—they have been shown to save more than they cost as they reduce weeks of UI paid and increase weeks of paid employment. Since the EUC RES/REA requirement was enacted, all states have fully implemented RES/REA programs and 3 million EUC claimants have received services. Based on an evaluation of regular REA program, there is evidence that, when combined with reemployment services similar to the EUC RES/REA program reemployment outcomes for claimants improve, claimants are more successful in returning to work sooner in jobs with higher wages, and duration of benefits are shorter. One study found that combining these services also increased reemployment by 20 percent and earnings of participants by 25 percent in the first year.

The Act also allowed states to expand "work-sharing", which will help prevent layoffs by encouraging employers to reduce hours for workers rather than eliminating their positions. Finally, the Act also allowed states to establish programs to encourage the long-term unemployed to start their own businesses - a significant reform for aspiring small business owners and entrepreneurs.

While there is more to be done, these reforms and many others have helped move the unemployment insurance program to a re-employment system.

VIII. Conclusion

The progress made since the depths of the recession in 2010 is a testament to the resilience of the American economy and the American people. Yet more must be done: there remain more than 10 million Americans unemployed, nearly 4 million of whom have been unemployed for more than 26 weeks. Thus far, the pain of the recession has been mitigated by the unemployment compensation programs, including EUC. Since Congress enacted the EUC program and offered 100 percent Federal funding of EB in June 2008, over 24 million people have been direct beneficiaries. The benefits have enabled the direct beneficiaries to search for jobs that utilize their skills, and encouraged the long-term unemployed to remain in the workforce continuing to search for work. The direct beneficiaries live in households that include more than 70 million people since 2008. The additional consumption afforded these households by EUC has kept millions of people out of poverty, 2.5 million in 2012 alone and over 11 million since 2008, and rippled through the economy to support growth.

Because Congress failed to act, EUC expired in the last week of December 2013. Approximately 1.3 million long-term unemployed workers lost their unemployment benefits at once at the end of December, and millions more will have no benefits after their initial 26 weeks of UI payments are exhausted during the course of 2014. Without an extension, 4.9 million workers will be affected by the end of 2014, and employment will be lower by 240,000 in 2014.

Appendix Table 1: Temporary Extended Benefit Programs

Name	Effective Dates	Weeks Payable	Financing
Temporary Unemployment Compensation (TUC)	Reachback to 06/57		Interest free loans to 17 participating states
PL 85-441	06/58 – 06/59	Up to 13	
Temporary Extended Unemployment Compensation (TEUC)	Reachback to 06/60		FUTA increase: 0.4% in 1962 0.25% in 1963
PL 87-6	04/61 – 06/62	Up to 13	
Temporary Compensation (TC) **PL 92-224**	No reachback		
PL 92-329	01/72 – 09/72	Up to 13	EUCA
	10/72 – 03/73	Up to 13	EUCA – FUTA increase 0.08% in 1973
Federal Supplemental Benefits (FSB)	No reachback	EB effective in all states through 12/77	
PL 93-572	01/75 – 03/75	Up to 13	EUCA
PL 94-12	03/75 – 09/75	Up to 26	EUCA
PL 94-45	10/75 – 12/75	Up to 26	EUCA
	01/76 – 03/77	Up to 13 or 26	EUCA
PL 95-19	04/77 – 01/78	Up to 13, beginning 05/77	General Revenue
Federal Supplemental Compensation (FSC)	Reachback to 06/82		
PL 97-248	09/82 – 12/82	Up to 6, 8, or 10	General Revenue
PL 97-424	01/83 – 03/83	Up to 8, 10, 12, 14, or 16	General Revenue
PL 98-21	04/83 – 09/83	Up to 8, 10, 12, or 14	General Revenue
PL 98-118	09/83 – 10/83	Up to 8, 10, 12, or 14	General Revenue
PL 98-135	10/83 – 03/85	Up to 8, 10, 12, or 14	General Revenue
PL 99-15	04/85 – 06/85	Phaseout	General Revenue
Emergency Unemployment Compensation (EUC)	Reachback to 02/91		
PL 102-164	11/91 – 02/92	Up to 13 or 20	EUCA
PL 102-244	02/92 – 06/92	Up to 26 or 33	EUCA
PL 102-318	06/92 – 09/93	Up to 20 or 26	General Revenue
PL 103-6	09/93 – 10/93	Up to 10 or 15	General Revenue
PL 103-152	10/93 – 02/94	Up to 7 or 13	EUCA
	02/94 – 04/94	Phaseout	EUCA
Temporary Extended Unemployment Compensation (TEUC)	Reachback to 03/01		
PL 107-147	03/02 – 12/02	Up to 13 or 26	EUCA
PL 108-1[1]	12/02 – 05/03	Up to 13 or 26	EUCA
PL 108-26	05/03 – 12/03	Up to 13 or 26	EUCA
	01/04 – 03/04	Phaseout	EUCA
Emergency Unemployment Compensation (EUC 08)	Reachback to 05/07		
PL 110-252	07/08 – 03/09	Up to 13	EUCA
PL 110-449	[2]	Up to 20 or 33	EUCA
PL 111-5	03/09 – 12/09	Up to 20 or 33	General Revenue
PL 111-92	[2]	Up to 20, 34, 47, or 53	General Revenue
PL 111-118	12/09 – 02/10	Up to 20, 34, 47, or 53	General Revenue
PL 111-144	02/10 – 04/10	Up to 20, 34, 47, or 53	General Revenue
PL 111-157	04/10 – 06/10	Up to 20, 34, 47, or 53	General Revenue
PL 111-205	06/10 – 11/10	Up to 20, 34, 47, or 53	General Revenue
PL 111-312	11/10 – 01/12	Up to 20, 34, 47, or 53	General Revenue
PL 112-78	01/12—02/12	Up to 20, 34, 47, or 53	General Revenue
PL 112-96	02/12—05/12	Up to 20, 34, 47, 53 or 63	General Revenue
PL 112-96	05/12—09/12	Up to 20, 34, 47, or 53	General Revenue
PL 112-96	09/12—12/12	Up to 14, 28, 37, or 47	General Revenue
PL 112-240	12/12—12/13	Up to 14, 28, 37, or 47	General Revenue

FUTA = Federal Unemployment Tax Act   **EUCA** = Extended Unemployment Compensation Account   Source: Department of Labor

[1] PL 108-11, which provided additional benefits (up to 39 or 52 weeks) to displaced airline and related workers under the TEUC-A program, is not included as it did not change the basic TEUC program.

[2] Expanded the number of weeks payable, but did not change effective dates

Appendix Table 2: Weeks and State Eligibility for Regular UI, EUC, and EB

Coverage	Program Length (weeks)	States Eligible[5]
UI	Up to 26[1]	all
EUC Tier 1	14	all
EUC Tier 2[2]	14	state unemployment rate > 6%
EUC Tier 3[3]	9	state unemployment rate > 7%
EUC Tier 4[4]	10	state unemployment rate > 9%
EB Option 1	13	state unemployment rate > 6.5% and higher than in at least one of the last three years
EB[5] Option 2	20	state unemployment rate > 8% and higher than in at least one of the last three years

1. Seven states currently offer less than 26 weeks: Arkansas (25), North Carolina (19), Florida (19), Georgia (18), Michigan (20), Missouri (20), and South Carolina (20). Montana provides 28 weeks. Massachusetts has a max of 30 weeks of regular UI *only* when there is no federal program of extended benefits. All other states, districts or territories offer 26 weeks.

2. As of November 2013, tier 2 is triggered on in 35 states, the District of Columbia, Puerto Rico, and the Virgin Islands.

3. As of November 2013, tier 3 is triggered on in 26 states, the District of Columbia, Puerto Rico, and the Virgin Islands.

4. As of November 2013, tier 4 is triggered on in 4 states, the Virgin Islands and the Puerto Rico.

5. The EB and EUC triggers reported are the current optional total unemployment rate (TUR) thresholds. The standard insured unemployment rate (IUR) triggers are usually not relevant, as they rarely qualify any state for EB or EUC; however, in February 2013 EUC became available in Alaska through the IUR trigger. States are either in option 1 or option 2 (or neither); recipients do not move sequentially through these options. States also must have in place a law that triggers EB on under the specified conditions. The three year reference is known as a, "look back" period; Congress extended this window to three from two years through the end of 2013. As of November 2013, EB is not triggered on in any state, the District of Columbia, Puerto Rico, or the Virgin Islands.

Source: Department of Labor

Appendix Table 3: Average Weekly UI Benefits, Maximum Weekly UI Benefits & Average UI Replacement Rate

State	Avg. Wkly Benefit 2013	Max Benefit 2013	Replacement rate (CY 2012)
Alabama	$208	$265	41.6%
Alaska	$250	$370	33.9%
Arizona	$220	$240	41.3%
Arkansas	$292	$451	51.7%
California	$305	$450	46.7%
Colorado	$366	$466	49.7%
Connecticut	$342	$591	44.0%
Delaware	$251	$330	42.4%
District of Columbia	$301	$359	39.1%
Florida	$232	$275	43.7%
Georgia	$269	$330	48.1%
Hawaii	$420	$534	54.3%
Idaho	$266	$357	46.7%
Illinois	$320	$413	40.3%
Indiana	$242	$390	38.6%
Iowa	$336	$396	53.0%
Kansas	$339	$456	53.4%
Kentucky	$292	$415	47.6%
Louisiana	$207	$247	39.1%
Maine	$289	$372	50.9%
Maryland	$331	$430	47.4%
Massachusetts	$490	$674	47.6%
Michigan	$293	$362	49.0%
Minnesota	$383	$393	48.7%
Mississippi	$193	$235	41.5%
Missouri	$242	$320	42.8%
Montana	$294	$446	47.0%
Nebraska	$282	$362	47.6%
Nevada	$314	$402	48.2%
New Hampshire	$300	$427	41.5%
New Jersey	$394	$624	52.2%
New Mexico	$306	$407	47.9%
New York	$308	$405	42.7%
North Carolina**	$283	$535	52.6%
North Dakota	$414	$516	51.0%
Ohio	$318	$413	44.6%
Oklahoma	$296	$386	50.1%
Oregon	$329	$524	47.7%
Pennsylvania	$357	$573	53.8%
Puerto Rico	$118	$133	36.2%
Rhode Island	$354	$566	48.9%
South Carolina	$253	$326	45.8%
South Dakota	$270	$333	48.0%
Tennessee	$241	$275	41.0%
Texas	$344	$440	49.6%
Utah	$350	$479	49.7%
Vermont	$316	$425	50.8%
Virgin Islands	$309	$491	N/A
Virginia	$303	$378	42.7%
Washington	$401	$604	49.9%
West Virginia	$276	$424	42.4%
Wisconsin	$272	$363	45.9%
Wyoming	$379	$459	49.4%
US	$310	$412	46.6%

Source: Department of Labor

References

Auerbach, Alan and Daniel Feenberg. 2000. "The Significance of Federal Taxes as Automatic Stabilizers." *Journal of Economic Perspectives* 14, no. 3:37-56.

Autor, David H. and Mark G. Duggan. 2003. "The Rise in the Disability Rolls and the Decline in Unemployment." *Quarterly Journal of Economics* 118, no. 1: 157-205.

Autor, David H., and Mark G. Duggan. 2006. "The Growth in the Social Security Disability Rolls: A Fiscal Crisis Unfolding." *Journal of Economic Perspectives* 20, no. 3: 71-96.

Black, Dan A., Jeffrey A. Smith, Mark C. Berger and Brett J. Noel. 2003. "Is the Threat of Reemployment Services More Effective than the Services Themselves? Evidence from Random Assignment in the UI System." *American Economic Review* 93, no. 4: 1313-1327.

Card, David and Phillip Levine. 2000. "Extended Benefits and the Duration of UI Spells: Evidence from the New Jersey Extended Benefit Program." *Journal of Public Economics* 78: 107-38.

Census Bureau. 2011. *Income, Poverty and Health Insurance Coverage in the United States: 2010."* Current Population Report. September.

Chetty, Raj. 2008. "Moral Hazard vs. Liquidity and Optimal Unemployment Insurance." *Journal of Political Economy* 116, no. 2: 173-234.

Chetty, Raj. 2013. "Economics is a Science." *New York Times.* October 21.

Congressional Budget Office. 2011. "Policies for Increasing Economic Growth and Employment in 2012 and 2013." Testimony by Douglas W. Elmendorf, Director. Prepared for Committee on the Budget, United States Senate.

Council of Economic Advisers. 2010. "The Economic Impact of Recent Temporary Unemployment Insurance Extensions," December.

Corson, Walter and Walter Nicholson. 1983. "An Analysis of UI Recipients' Unemployment Spells." Unemployment Insurance Occasional Paper, No. 83-1, U.S. Department of Labor, Employment and Training Administration.

Feldstein, Martin. 1974. "Unemployment Compensation: Adverse Incentives and Distributional Anomalies." *National Tax Journal* 27, no. 2: 231-244.

Foote, Christopher L., Kristopher S. Gerardi, Lorenz Goette, and Paul S. Willen. 2009. "Reducing Foreclosures." Federal Reserve Bank of Boston working paper.

Gruber, Jonathan. 1997. "The Consumption Smoothing Benefits of Unemployment Insurance." *American Economic Review* 87, no. 1: 192-205.

Hanna, James and Zina Turney. 1990. "UI Research Exchange: The Economic Impact of the Nevada Claimant Employment Program." UI Occasional Paper, no. 90-4. Washington, DC: U.S. Department of Labor, Employment and Training Administration, Unemployment Insurance Service.

Hutchens, Robert. 1981. "Distributional Equity in the Unemployment Insurance System." *Industrial and Labor Relations Review* 34, no. 3: 377-385.

Jacobson, Louis. 2009. "Strengthening One-Stop Career Centers: Helping More Unemployed Workers Find Jobs and Build Skills." Hamilton Project Discussion Paper.

Katz, Lawrence F. and Bruce D. Meyer. 1990. "Unemployment Insurance, Recall Expectations, and Unemployment Outcomes." *The Quarterly Journal of Economics* 105, no. 4: 973-1002.

Kroft, Kory and Matthew Notowidigdo. 2011. "Should Unemployment Insurance Vary with the Local Unemployment Rate? Theory and Evidence." Working Paper

Krueger, Alan, and Andreas Mueller. In progress. "Applications for Disability Insurance and the Exhaustion of Unemployment Insurance Benefits: New Evidence from a Survey of Unemployed Workers."

Meyer, Bruce D. 1990. "Unemployment Insurance and Unemployment Spells." *Econometrica* 58, no.4: 757–782.

Meyer, Bruce D. 1995. "Lessons from the U.S. Unemployment Insurance Experiments." *Journal of Economic Literature* 33, no. 1: 91-131.

Meyer, Bruce D., Wallace K.C. Mok, James X. Sullivan. 2009. "The Under-Reporting of Transfers in Household Surveys: Its Nature and Consequences." NBER Working Paper 15181. Cambridge, MA: National Bureau of Economic Research. July.

Michaelides, Marios and Jacob Benus. 2010. "Are Self-Employment Training Programs Effective? Evidence from Project GATE." IMPAQ International and University of Maryland – College Park. Commissioned by the U.S. Department of Labor.

Poe-Yamagata, Eileen, Jacob Benus, Nicholas Bill, Hugh Carrington, Marios Michaelides, and Ted Shen. 2011. "Impact of the Reemployment and Eligibility Assessment (REA) Initiative." IMPAQ International. Commissioned by the U.S. Department of Labor.

Rothstein, Jesse. 2011. "Unemployment Insurance and Job Search in the Great Recession." *Brookings Papers on Economic Activity.*

Rothstein, Jesse and Rob Valletta. 2013. "Scraping By: Responses to Unemployment Insurance Exhaustion in the Aftermath of the Great Recession." *Presentation to All-California Labor Conference, September 9.*

Schmieder, Johannes, Till von Wachter, and Stefan Bender. Forthcoming. "The Effects of Extended Unemployment Insurance over the Business Cycle: Evidence from Regression Discontinuity Estimates over Twenty Years." *Quarterly Journal of Economics*.